The Social Lives of Animals

A CHAPTER BOOK

BY KATHERINE GLEASON

children's press®

A Division of Scholastic Inc.
New York   Toronto   London   Auckland   Sydney
Mexico City   New Delhi   Hong Kong
Danbury, Connecticut

For Jean Berko and Andrew M. Gleason, my parents

ACKNOWLEDGMENTS

The author would like to thank all the scientists whose exciting work has made this book possible. In particular, thanks and best wishes go to Gerald S. Wilkinson, professor of zoology, University of Maryland at College Park; Iain D. Couzin, postdoctoral researcher in ecology and evolutionary biology, Princeton University, Princeton, N.J.; Ben Wilson, marine biologist, Marine Mammal Research Unit, University of British Columbia, Vancouver, Canada; and Hugo J. Rainey, School of Biology, University of St. Andrews, St. Andrews, Scotland.

Library of Congress Cataloging-in-Publication Data

Gleason, Katherine.
  The social lives of animals : a chapter book / by Katherine Gleason.
    p. cm. — (True tales)
  Includes bibliographical references and index.
  ISBN 0-516-25188-0 (lib. bdg.)   0-516-25458-8 (pbk.)
  1. Social behavior in animals—Juvenile literature. I. Title. II. Series.
  QL775.G56 2005
  591.56--dc22
                    2004028458

1 2 3 4 5 6 7 8 9 10 R 14 13 12 11 10 09 08 07 06 05

CONTENTS

INTRODUCTION

Biologists study living things. Some biologists look at animals and their social behavior. **Social behavior** includes all the things that an animal does as part of a group. For example, some animals hunt in groups. Other animals work together to avoid being eaten.

Gerald Wilkinson found out that after vampire bats hunt, they actually share their food with other bats. Iain Couzin discovered that army ants follow rules and work together when they hunt. Ben Wilson studies **herring**, a kind of fish. He found out that groups of herring **communicate** with each other in unusual ways. In Africa, Hugo Rainey discovered that small groups of birds listen to what their monkey neighbors have to say. Listening keeps these birds from becoming another animal's next meal.

Read about these exciting discoveries and learn about the people who study animal social life.

CHAPTER ONE

BATS
THAT SHARE

It is night. A vampire bat walks along the ground using its wings and back legs. It moves toward a group of sleeping horses. It jumps on a horse and hangs from the animal's mane.

Vampire bat

The bat picks a spot on the horse's neck and makes a tiny bite. The bat's teeth are so sharp that the horse does not feel the **wound**. The bat laps blood from the wound with its tongue for about half an hour.

A vampire bat laps blood from the leg of a chicken.

Vampire bats need to drink a blood meal regularly. If a vampire bat does not find blood two nights in a row, it will begin to starve.

Biologist Gerald Wilkinson knows a lot about vampire bats. Gerald and his team of researchers spent five years studying them in Costa Rica, a small country in Central America.

Before he left for Costa Rica, Gerald already knew that a mother vampire bat sometimes shares her blood meal with her **pup**. She does this by **regurgitating** (re-GUR-juh-tayting) some of the blood that she has drunk. Gerald wanted to find out if vampire bats share only with their relatives. Or will a vampire bat share with any bat that is hungry?

To find an answer, Gerald and his team studied three groups of vampire bats. These bats have **roosts** inside large tree hollows. The hollows stretch as high as 30 feet (9 meters).

Vampire bats sleep hanging upside down.

Gerald studying vampire bats in a tree hollow

Each tree was home to between five and twenty adult female bats and their pups. Three or four male bats shared these trees, too.

Each hollow tree has one opening through which the bats come and go. The researchers stretched a net over the opening. They caught each bat and put several colored bands on one forearm. The bands allowed the researchers to **identify** the bats.

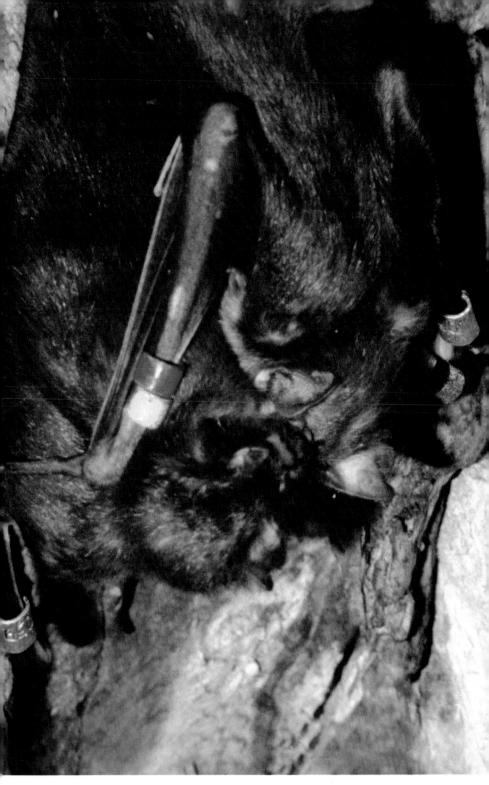

The bands on the bats are covered with a special kind of shiny tape so the researchers can see them in dim light.

To watch the bats, the researchers laid a plastic **tarp** on the ground at the bottom of the hollow. They wore hats to protect themselves from bat droppings, or **guano** (GWAH-noh). They also wore respirators so they would not breathe in a **fungus** (FUN-gis) that grows on bat guano. The fungus can make you sick. One researcher lay on the tarp, watching the bats through binoculars. A second researcher sat at the foot of the tree and wrote down what the bat watcher saw.

A hungry bat asks for food by grooming a bat that has fed. First the hungry bat licks the other bat under the wing. Then the hungry bat licks the other bat's face and lips. If the bat that has fed agrees, it regurgitates some of its blood meal into the hungry bat's mouth.

The researchers noticed that most of the food sharing was between mother bats and

A group of vampire bats inside a tree hollow

their pups. They also saw adult females feed the pups of other bats. They saw adult females feed other adult females, and a few times they saw male bats regurgitate blood for their pups. Overall, the researchers noted that bats share with both their relatives and their roost mates.

After studying a group of bats in the lab, Gerald found that vampire bats have a buddy system. The bats form buddy pairs. The two bats in a buddy pair go to each

These hyenas are sharing the day's catch.

other if they are hungry. The bat that has fed gives food to its hungry buddy. This system helps both the hungry bat and the giver. The hungry bat is saved from starving. The giver can count on its buddy to repay the favor in the future.

Food sharing between **unrelated** animals is rare. Only bats, wild dogs, hyenas, some **primates**, and, of course, humans share. Sharing food helps the animals that are hungry. It also helps the animals that share. The giver today will get help from its buddy tomorrow.

Sharing ice cream cones with friends

CHAPTER TWO

RULES OF THE ROAD

Two hundred thousand army ants march across the rain forest floor. Their feet rustle as they move. They are searching for food. In one hour, these ants will catch about 3,000 grasshoppers and other bugs. In ten hours, they will catch 30,000 tasty bugs to eat. The ants hunt like this every day.

Army ant

These army ants are eating a katydid.

The ants are very good at grabbing their **prey** and bringing it back to the nest. Amazingly enough, the ants are practically blind. Even so, they make it back. In addition, they return to the nest without running into each other or creating traffic jams. And they do all this with no stop signs, traffic lights, or police officers to direct them.

Biologists Iain Couzin and Nigel Franks went to Panama, a country in Central America, to study the traffic patterns of army ants. They already knew that army ants

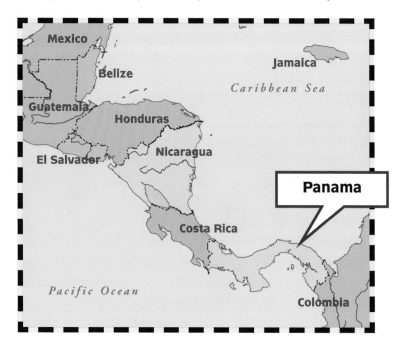

A researcher looking at a trail of ants

follow their own roads. The roads that the ants use are not like the roads that people build. They are not made of cement and blacktop. The ants make their roads from smelly **chemicals**.

Each ant helps to make the chemical road. When the ants first leave the nest, they move in a big group called a swarm. The ants at the front of the swarm start making the road as they slowly move forward. Then each ant follows the trail of chemicals to leave and return to the nest.

A nest of army ants

Because the ants can't see well, they rely on their sense of smell to get around. To keep from getting lost, each ant wants to stay close to the center of the chemical road, where the scent is strongest. Since so many ants are on the move at once, the ants can't always do this. In fact, the ants end up forming three lanes of traffic. Ants leaving the nest march along one of the two outside lanes. Once an ant finds food along the trail, it hurries back to the nest along the center lane.

Iain and Nigel wanted to find out how **colonies** of ants organize themselves in this way. They wanted to know how the ants keep their traffic running so smoothly.

The scientists found the answers to their questions by using a computer. First they videotaped the ants. Then they played the tape into a computer. They used a special computer program that Iain created. The computer program looks at the pictures of the ants and follows the movement of each individual ant in the group.

An ant colony

After careful study, Iain and Nigel discovered that each ant follows two simple rules. First, when moving away from the nest, an ant turns sharply to get out of the way of others that are returning to the nest.

Iain looks at his computer screen to see the trails made by the ants.

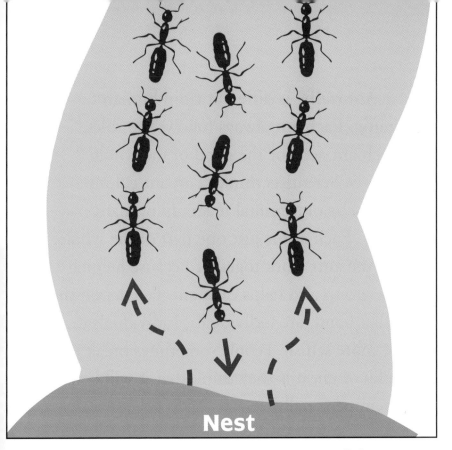

Nest

Ants leaving the nest turn to stay out of the way of others returning to the nest.

Then the ant turns back to continue along the road. Later, when heading back to the nest, the ant does not turn. It stays near the center of the scent-marked road.

These simple rules, followed by hundreds of thousands of ants, cause the marching ants to form three traffic lanes. This traffic pattern allows the colony of ants to hunt and travel without bumping into each other or getting stuck in traffic jams.

Ant traffic is different from human traffic. Each ant always follows the rules. Each ant acts for the good of the whole colony. Scientists think of an ant colony almost as one animal made up of many parts. Each ant is just one part of the whole. All the ants work together because helping the group also helps each ant. People, on the other hand, are individuals. Individuals can be more selfish. People sometimes break the rules or cheat if they think that it will help them personally.

Some traffic jams are caused by people not following traffic rules.

CHAPTER THREE

BLOWING BUBBLES

Late one night, biologist Ben Wilson sat in his lab. He was alone with a tank of thirty herring. As an **experiment**, he was about to play dolphin sounds to these fish. He wanted to see how the fish would react to the sounds of a **predator**.

Before he turned on the tape player, he heard something strange. It sounded as if someone was blowing air through rubbery lips. *Brrrrr.* Was someone playing a joke on him? He froze in place, and the sound came again. *Brrrrr.* This time he was sure the sound came from inside the fish tank. Imagining that something had

Ben Wilson

Herring swimming in a group

Ben scoops a herring from the tank.

fallen into the tank, he switched on the light. He saw only fish startled by the brightness.

Ben knew that herring store air inside their bodies. They store the air, which helps them float, in their **swim bladders**. In herring, the swim bladder has two openings. One opening leads into the stomach. The other opening is a thin tube that ends near the fish's **anus** (AYE-nus). Ben wondered if the noise came from air moving out of the swim bladder. To find out, he held a dead fish underwater and squeezed it. A stream of bubbles poured from the fish's rear end. At the same time, he heard the sound again.

To find out more, Ben and his team set up special underwater microphones in a tank of fish. They also used special video cameras to record the fish in the dark. Ben had noticed that the fish make noise mostly at night, so the team worked at night. When they watched tapes of the herring, they saw little streams of bubbles coming from the

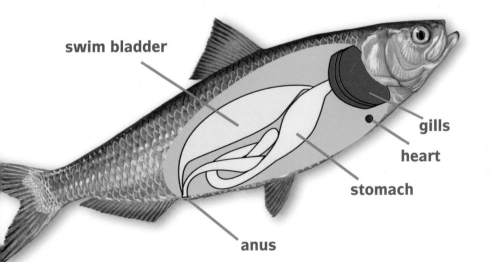

swim bladder

gills

heart

stomach

anus

Some of the equipment used to record the fish sounds

fishes' rear ends. The bubbles appeared at the same time as the sound. To the scientists, it seemed as if the fish were passing gas!

Ben wondered why herring make this noise. He was pretty sure the bubbles coming out of the fish were not **methane**. Methane is the gas animals pass when they **digest** food. He still thought the bubbles were probably air coming from the swim bladder.

To test if he was right, Ben did an experiment. He stopped feeding a group of fish. Ben found out that the fish that were not fed made just as many bubbles and just as much noise as the fish that did eat. He concluded that the bubbles were not caused by the fish passing methane.

Next, Ben wanted to find out if fear would change how much sound the fish made. In another experiment, he set up a container full of dogfish sharks near a tank of herring. Dogfish sharks eat herring. Water

Herring swimming in the ocean

Dogfish shark

from the shark tank was fed into the herring tank. Although the herring could smell the sharks, the fish continued to make their noise. In fact, they made the same amount of noise as fish that were not sharing water with sharks. Ben concluded that herring do not blow bubbles because of fear.

Then Ben and his team noticed that the more herring there were in a tank, the more

noise they made. Each fish in a crowded tank produced more noise and more bubbles than each individual fish in less crowded tanks. Perhaps the herring use their sounds to communicate with one another.

Because the sound is high-pitched, other fish in the ocean cannot hear it. Herring, on the other hand, can hear high-pitched sounds. The researchers think the herring make these sounds to help them stay together in a **school** and avoid predators at night when it is too dark to see.

Because herring seem to use their sense of hearing, the researchers worry about all the noise made by boats. Under the water, boat

engines can be very loud. These noises may keep herring from hearing each other and staying safe from predators. The researchers also are concerned about the animals that prey on herring. Marine mammals such as dolphins may be bothered by loud boat noises, too. The researchers think that dolphins may use sound to help them locate schools of herring. Boat noise may make it hard for dolphins to hear the herring and catch their meals. Noise could be upsetting the balance of life in the ocean and making survival harder for all the animals that live there.

Dolphin

Engines on fishing boats make the ocean a noisy place for herring and dolphins.

CHAPTER FOUR

LISTENING IN

Biologist Hugo Rainey pushed the "play" button on his tape player. Earlier in the day, he had made recordings of Diana monkeys in the jungle. When the tape started, he could not hear the monkeys right away. Instead, he heard the loud honks of birds. The birds he heard were yellow-casqued hornbills. Sometimes when the monkeys called out, the hornbills did, too.

Hugo Rainey

Diana monkeys live in Africa.

All hornbills have helmet-like structures on top of their bills. These structures make their calls sound louder.

When he heard the noisy hornbills, Hugo became curious. He knew that some types of **mammals**, such as lemurs, listen and respond to the calls of other animals. He was not sure if birds could do that, too. He wanted to discover exactly when the hornbills called out.

Hugo wanted to find out if the hornbills understood different Diana monkey calls. Diana monkeys make one sound that means an eagle is coming. They make a different sound that means a leopard is coming.

Hornbills and Diana monkeys often feed near each other at fruit trees. Both hornbills and Diana monkeys are prey for eagles. Leopards, on the other hand, do not eat hornbills. Hugo guessed that the hornbills might react strongly to the Diana monkey's eagle call. He also guessed that the hornbills would not pay attention to the leopard call. To find out if he was right, he set up an experiment.

In the Ivory Coast, a country in Africa, Hugo walked through the forest to find a group of hornbills. At first this was easy.

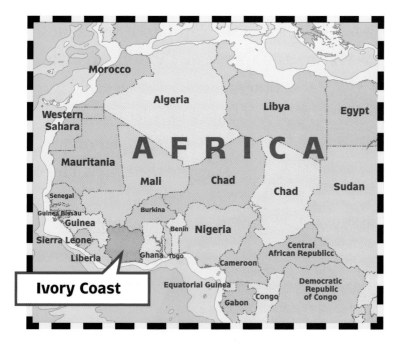

Later, the hornbills moved and he had to walk as much as 16 miles (25 kilometers) a day to find them.

Hugo spent a year and a half in the jungle with the hornbills.

Once Hugo found a group of hornbills, he placed a speaker about 50 yards (46 meters) from the birds. Then he played them some sounds.

First, Hugo wanted to know how hornbills act when an eagle is coming. On his tape player, he played the high pitched sound of an eagle. The hornbills called out a warning. It was almost as if they were shouting to each other, "Look out! An eagle is coming. Don't let it eat you!" Because eagles often surprise their prey, Hugo thinks that the hornbill calls may also serve as a warning

Eagle

40

to eagles. The hornbills may also be saying, "I see you, eagle. You can't sneak up and catch me now!"

Next, Hugo wanted to see what the hornbills would do when they heard a leopard. He played the roar of a leopard, and the hornbills did not call out to each other. Because leopards do not eat hornbills, the hornbills had no reason to fear them.

Then, Hugo played some Diana monkey calls to the hornbills. The monkey call that warns of an eagle sounds a lot like the call that warns of a leopard. Both monkey calls are loud barking sounds. Even though the monkey calls are similar, the hornbills understood the difference between them.

Leopard

Diana monkeys live in groups that have from five to fifty members.

When Hugo played the monkey call that warns of an eagle, the hornbills called out, too. They screeched to let all the other hornbills know an eagle was coming. When Hugo played the call that warns of a leopard, the hornbills were quiet.

With his experiment, Hugo proved that hornbills listen to Diana monkeys. He also proved that hornbills understand the difference between two different monkey calls. This is the first time a scientist has proved that a bird can understand a mammal.

Hornbills

GLOSSARY

anus (AYE-nus) the opening at the end of the digestive tract

biologist a person who studies living things

chemical something that takes up space, has weight, and is used in chemistry

colony a group of animals that live together

communicate to share information with another

digest to break down food so it can be used by the body

experiment a test to find out if something is true

fungus (FUN-gis) a plantlike living thing that doesn't have leaves or flowers and that doesn't make its own food

guano (GWAH-noh) bat droppings

herring a type of fish that lives in the Atlantic and Pacific oceans

identify to be able to tell what something is or who someone is

mammal an animal that is warm-blooded and feeds milk to its young

methane a type of gas made during digestion

predator an animal that hunts and eats other animals

prey an animal that is hunted and eaten by other animals

primate a member of a group of mammals that includes humans, apes, and monkeys

pup a baby bat

regurgitate (re-GUR-juh-tayt) to throw up partly eaten food

roost a place for rest or sleep

school a group of fish that stays together

social behavior the way people or animals act around each other

swim bladder an organ in a fish where air is kept

tarp heavy cloth that is used as a covering

unrelated not part of the same family

wound a cut or other injury

FIND OUT MORE

Bats That Share
www.nationalgeographic.com/kids/creature_feature/0110
/vampirebats.html
Find out more about vampire bats.

Rules of the Road
www.ex.ac.uk/bugclub/raiders.html
Learn more about army ants and how they hunt.

Blowing Bubbles
www.zoology.ubc.ca/~bwilson/herring.html
Hear the sounds herring make when they communicate.

Listening In
http://news.bbc.co.uk/media/audio/39912000/rm/_3991
2367_birdies.ram
Listen to Hugo Rainey talk about his research on Diana
monkeys and hornbills.

More Books to Read

The Fascinating World of Ants by Angels Julivert, Barron's
Educational Series, 1991

*Fish Sleep but Don't Shut Their Eyes and Other Amazing
Facts About Ocean Creatures (Speedy Facts)* by Melvin
Berger, Scholastic Reference, 2004

Safari Guide!: Scouting for Wildlife in Africa by Robyn
Brode, Barron's Educational Series, 2002

Vampire Bats (Naturebooks) by Patrick Merrick, Childs
World, 2000

INDEX

PHOTO CREDITS

MEET THE AUTHOR

 Katherine Gleason has worked in children's publishing as an editor, project manager, and author. She has written numerous books for children and a few for adults, as well. She particularly enjoys writing and reading books about animals, ancient cultures, and faraway places. Her love of travel has taken her all over the world, and she has, in fact, visited all seven of Earth's continents. Gleason lives in New York City with her cat, Elphaba.